More Snapshots

From My Family Album

Daveda Gruber

©2007 by Daveda Gruber.
All Rights reserved. No part of this book may be reproduced, stored in retrieval system or transmitted in any firm by ant means without the prior permission of the publishers.
Exceptions are by a reviewer who may quote brief passages in a review to be printed in a newspaper, magazine or journal.
ISBN: 978-0-6151-8648-1

I dedicate this book
to my
Family and friends.

Table of Contents Page 1

Being Myself..6
Family.. 7
My Wonderful Mommy...8
To My Husband...9
In Dream When You Come.....................................10
With a Smile...12
Daughter..16
Her Wish..18
I Am..20
Dear Daddy In Heaven...22
Happy Father's Day...24
Growing Up..25
Growing Up II...27
Growing Up III..30
Growing Up IV..34
Auntie Bea...37
Shedding of a Tear..41
Tropical Storm..42
Daveda..43
The Pictures...44
Heaven on Earth...46
We Cannot Forget...49
Shari the Lionhearted..51
You Will Never Rule Me..54
Render a Vow...56
Happy Mother's Day..58
Mother's Day..59
Dear Santa...60
What Children Say...62
True Love...65

Table of Contents Page 2

Mirror of Me	66
Flowers from a Friend	69
Happy Birthday Pat	70
Four Letters	72
The Mirror	74
By Your Side	76
A Friend like You	78
Open Your Mind	79
Scorpio Season	80
Who I Am	82
Love in America	83
Marriage	84
The Brilliance of Love	85
Such Love	86
For Eternity	87
Take Me Away	88
Hopes For You	90
Souls Entwined	91
Hearts Aglow	92
As She Gazed	94
Immigration	96
For The Future	98
It Won't Get Me	101
Road of Life	102
Myself	103
Ones Worth	104
The Book	105
Desired Splendor	106
Husband and Lover	108
Glasses of Love	110

Being Myself
(Senryu Suite)

Personality
I possess belongs to me
I set myself free

~~*~~

I will always be
Me in whatever I do
Who I am is me

~~*~~

I cannot be changed
I believe in who I am
Accept who I am

~*~

Family

As we see the seasons of our lives, go by,
There is no doubt, on others we do rely.
Years pass and our loved ones tend to move along.
Before we know, there is nowhere we belong.

~~*~~

A family tree has branches, which stretch out.
A flash in time, new seeds have begun to sprout.
Days turn into years, which pass before our eyes,
As we realize the tree has aged and dies.

~~*~~

Enjoy the magnificence of the splendor,
Relish the gifts of growing seeds so tender.
Take time to touch the branches getting brittle.
Behold memories of when you were little.

~~*~~

There is magic in the delights as we grow.
Take part in this enchanting and wondrous show.
Hold on tight and refuse to never let go.
You will find in family, all you Must know!

~*~

My Wonderful Mommy
(Acrostic Rhymed)

Helping hands you have always given,
Always, for your children you've been driven.
Preparing meals; the best on this earth,
Pride in knowing your undeniable worth.
Yesterdays have gone by all too fast.

Birthdays come and many have past.
I treasure each year, spent with you.
Reminding me, of your love so true.
This year, may you have a perfect day,
Hoping that I may help in some way.
Daveda, your daughter, dedicates to you,
A poem that you are meant to read into.
Yes, dear mommy, my love will always be true!

To My Husband
(Acrostic-Rhymed)

Having a wonderful husband like you,
As beautiful dreams, for me have come true.
Preparing to live the rest of our lives together,
Pleasing each other in good and bad weather.
Yesterday's dream now today's expectation.

Forever, my love; I give without hesitation,
Assuring you what we hold is real;
That there is truth in what we feel.
Happiness in being as one we will find.
Every moment together; our lives entwined.
Relishing in the affection we show;
Satisfaction in pleasing the other as we grow.

Darling, I cherish the day I found you.
A love like this; is found only by a few.
You, my dear, are my wishes come true!

~*~

In Dreams When You Come
In memory of my daughter, Lanie (1968-2004)

Dear daughter, here comes that time of year,
Where in the depths of my soul, there is pain.
Even though you are gone; I love you still.
My tears for you, on my heart, have left a stain.

~~*~~

To comprehend, the death of a daughter;
Is difficult to grasp, for this mother of yours.
As our birthdays approach, I die a little more.
For this slow death of mine, there are no cures.

~~*~~

As we mature, and age comes with time;
I am traveling closer, to be with you, once again.
You could have stayed longer, if you had wished.
Only you, dear daughter, could be the one to explain.

~~*~~

I hear your laughter and I see your face;
In dreams when you come to me.
Is it in heaven, where you cry no more?
Have you, like the butterflies, been set free?

~~*~~

Can you feel the awesome ocean's waves of blue?
Do you dance with dolphins, that you loved so?
Child of mine, who became a beautiful woman;
As an angel in heaven, you must surely glow.

~*~

With A Smile

In my husband's office, which is in the house,
I noticed carpet was wet and told my spouse.
"Must have been your little dog," my husband said.
I replied, "My poodle! Come check this instead!"

~~*~~

He looked at the carpet: knew something was wrong.
Called furnace people and said don't take too long!
One guy came and took a look; things were a mess.
"I need more men for this job," he did confess.

~~*~~

Well, we had the water turned off, which was not good.
A big expense this would be, we understood.
More workers came and said, furnace had to go.
You'll have no water or air; that you must know!

We booked a hotel room with a Jacuzzi.
About where I stay, I am very choosy.
No dogs allowed, even one that weighs three pounds.
From the house and hotel, I was doing rounds.

~~*~~

Out of home expenses, insurance covered.
We could dine out, every night, we discovered.
First night, I ordered filet mignon not spiced.
Well, petit or large, the big one would be nice.

Home we went, so the dog could have some fun.
Bits of meat I gave to her, after her run.
I felt bad leaving, to go to the hotel,
Still, I knew in my heart that all would be well.

~~*~~

Next morning rushed home, my poodle was just fine.
Gave her filet mignon, on which she could dine.
Man said, " Water tank won't fit with new heater."
"You can buy one without tank from the dealer."

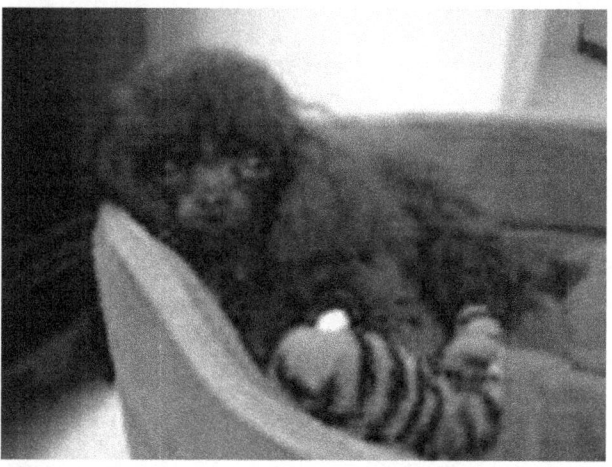

Much more efficient, this system would now be.
My husband would be paying, would not cost me!
Later, went back to the hotel for an hour.
Relax in Jacuzzi; wash hair in shower.

~~*~~

We went out to eat, the large salmon I picked,
No spices or glaze my husband did predict.
You guessed, my dog thinks salmon is nice treat.
So, I went back home and gave her some to eat.

~~*~~

Next day, the house was ready, time to go back.
Some ingredients for cooking, I did lack.
Meat, salmon, broccoli and carrots cut up,
Boiled brown rice and peas, mixed all up for the pup.

~~*~~

She was so happy with her dinner that night.
Had much to freeze in containers to delight.
I made hotdogs and beans; we ate with a smile.
Lady Godiva, my poodle, ate in style.

~*~

Daughter

Pleasure has been bestowed upon me.
I watch my Lovely daughter napping.
Enjoying the opportunity,
To be able to smile, recapping.

~~*~~

As I look at her, I am beguiled,
A gift, for such a very short time.
The love given to me, by my child,
I relish one more day; she's all mine.

~~*~~

In my heart I know, she cannot stay.
I'll wait till I have her near again.
She must go back home in one short day.
There will be inevitable pain.

~~*~~

She's all grown up, to those who meet her.
I brought to life such a precious pearl.
What ever in this life may occur,
Shayna, always be my baby girl!

~*~

Her Wish

She tossed the coin into wishing well, for all to see.
She made a wish, for love to last for eternity.
The love she knew was powerful and so very strong.
Love had found the special place, where her heart did belong.

~~***~~

Many times, she thought she had found love
before this day.
Now she knew, that true love had finally found its
way.
Her heart sang out in praise for the ecstasy of
love.
God had at long last sent this love, from heaven
above.

~~***~~

Now, all that she wished for was to make this
moment last.
This time, she knew her desire for him was
unsurpassed.
All that she ever wanted and needed in her life;
To live happily for eternity, as his wife.

~*~

I Am
(Double Ethree)

I
Am a
Woman who
Enjoys being
A person who is
First-rate, inside and out.
I believe in lending a hand.
Helping others makes me feel so good,
When things are possible to accomplish.

~~***~~

To be able to give and receive love,
I must love myself for who I am.
To be the best that I can be;
Is what I strive for in life.
Loving my fellow man,
The right thing to do;
This much I know.
This is me;
Who I
Am.

~***~

Dear Daddy In Heaven
to my daddy ...Mackey (Maxwell)

You told me that I was your special girl.
Over your head, you loved to make me swirl.
Late at night, you would let me watch TV.
On your lap, I loved it when you held me.

<<<>>>*<<<>>>

Daddy in Heaven, are you sleeping now?
As I hold back tears, I will not allow.
Daddy you told me, "Daveda don't cry,"
"For it has come the time that I must die."

<<<>>>*<<<>>>

Please Daddy; I cannot hold back my tears,
Even though it has been so many years.
I brought to life, more children, did you see?
Daddy, why is life still so hard on me?

<<<>>>*<<<>>>

So many times, I wished you were still here,
To take away all my troubles and fears.
Oh Daddy; all of the answers you had.
You knew how to make your little girl glad.

<<>>*<<>>

So, dear Daddy; I ask you to oversee,
Take care of my first child taken from me.
Also, watch over Sharon, my sister,
You understand, how much, I do miss her.

<<<>>>*<<<>>

I have so many decisions to make.
My tattered heart will most certainly break.
From heaven, could you send me answers, please?
Dear Daddy, help my heart to be at ease.

>>>*<<<

Happy Father's Day!
(Spanish Huitain)

I hope your day goes very well.
A unique dad that all can see;
You are, as far as I can tell.
Being the best that you can be;
Be certain your sons can agree.
Caring for them in your own way,
You are so loved; I guarantee.
So, from me, Happy Father's Day!

>>>*<<<

Growing Up
to my sisters ...Gloria and the late Sharon

I grew up in a great big city,
I thought it was extremely pretty.
Three sisters were always together.
As one, just like birds of a feather.

<>

I walked with my sisters down the street
Never strangers, did we stop to greet.
As three little sisters, we did go,
Holding hands and skipping toe to toe.

Every day we heard some people say,
Three little sisters are on their way,
Must have somewhere important to go.
We just liked skipping, but who would know?

**I was the eldest, hair blond and light,
Next, my sister with hair dark as night.
Strawberry blond, the youngest and last,
Together, we always had a blast.**

**Around my apartment house we played,
A playground of a paved lane we made.
We played many games, that we all knew,
Through many days at play, we three grew.**

<>

Growing Up ....part II

Beside the apartment house, where I grew,
To the paved lane, all of the children flew.
We ran to play games we loved to no end.
Red light, green light, hours of fun we would spend.

One child was chosen, to start as the light.
She would decide the next given the right.
First in line, asked is the light red or green?
If green, then run till you hear a loud scream!

<>

Red was yelled out and then you had to stop.
The winner was who, got first, to the top.
So, all of the children did scream and yell.
"I want to run, if you don't let I'll tell."

A lady had a window near the lane.
To the children, she would always complain.
You better stop all of that noise down there!
We would sing, "na na na na, we don't care!"

<>

**As children, we knew no end to our games.
To the old woman, we would call out names.
Buckets of water on us she did dump!
From the lane where we played, we sure did jump!**

<>

Growing Up (part III)

My sisters and I went outside to play,
Children would yell, three little sisters, yeah!
Three more, do make a game more fun, you see,
More fun, to play endless games, filled with glee.

What would be a good game to start the day?
Hide and seek, would make all the children stay.
Enie meanie miney, moe you are it!
Gloria, if you're it you cannot quit!

<>

Gloria was not always a good sport.
For at playing fairly, she fell a bit short.
Hid her eyes, started to count to twenty.
Peeking, decided that must be plenty.

<>

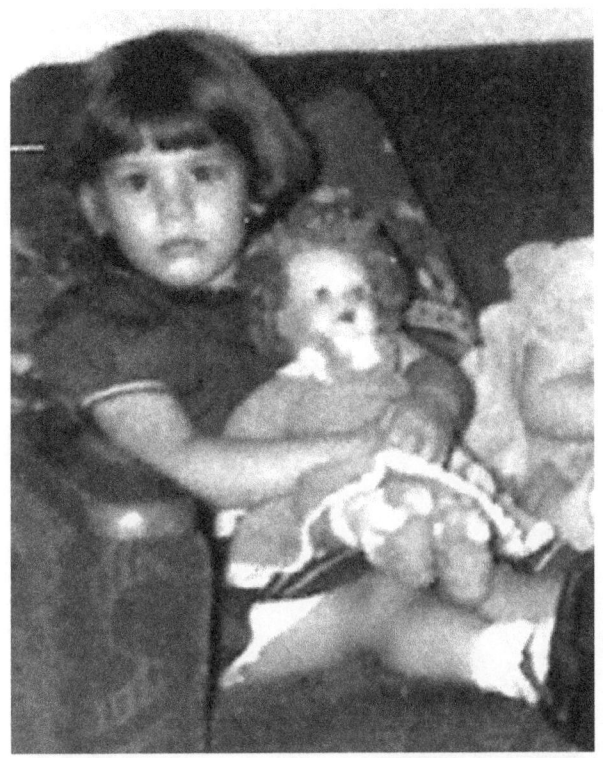

Gloria yelled, ready or not here I come!
Seeing where most had hid, she would find some.
Never told she cheated, would not be right.
I knew better, could only start a fight.

<>

One left hidden, Sharon my young sister.
Gloria peeking had some how missed her.
Gloria was it, till she found us all.
What would be, if she could not find, one small?

<>

**The first was doomed to be "it" the next round.
Maybe Sharon's hiding place could be found.
Sharon was hiding in the locker room;
She had found a place dark and full of gloom.**

<>

The game was over; Sharon was asleep.
Sharon was sleeping, curled up in a heap.
Getting his bike, from basement was a man;
Sharon saw his shadow and out she ran!

<>

"There's a monster in the basement," she shouted!
She saw the monster no one dared doubt it
No one was brave enough to check and see
Monsters lived in the basement, we did agree

<>

Growing up (Part IV)

With sisters to play with, we had built in friends.
Wearing dresses for parties; there were no ends.
So, three little sisters were ready for fun.
When dressed so pretty; we knew never to run.

My grandmother's house was wide open to all.
Our cousin Maureen came along for a ball.
Christmas parties were always a superb treat,
Lots of presents and delicious food to eat.

For birthday parties, we adored getting dressed,
Playing together waiting for the first guest.
Hats and whistles made three sisters excited.
Laughter and joy, eager for those invited.

Whatever the occasion, three sisters knew,
We would always be together as we grew.
For one and other, we would always be there,
Strong bond between us, of that we were aware.

<>

Auntie Bea
in memory of a dear aunt ...Beatrice

She was quite a rebel in her hey day;
Special even when her hair turned to grey.
For driving a car she sure was gifted,
All did know when her garage door lifted;
It was going to be a big matter!
All the people on the street would scatter.
Auntie Beatrice was going to back out;
Run for your lives, all the neighbors did shout!

∾∾∾******∾∾∾

If you saw this lady behind the wheel,
She was the queen of the automobile.
Always using her car for speed and force,
Driving just like she was on a race course.
Her elbow out the window of the car,
My auntie Beatrice was a reigning star.
A terror in a car she was known as;
Oh, my auntie sure had lots of pizzazz!

∾∾***∾∾

You see Killer was the nickname she had,
If you met her, you knew, don't make her mad.
Those she liked had a place inside her heart.
If on her "black list", she'd tear you apart!
Such great love for me had been ignited.
That sure made me feel awfully delighted.

~~***~~

When we found out the end was very near,
My cousin, an only child, had much fear.
Hospital was were we stayed every day.
Smiles for Auntie Bea we still did display.
We understood the end was nearing fast,
I was with her, the night, which was her last.

~~***~~

My cousin, Maureen, left to get some clothes.
My strength would stay, that was clear, I suppose.
The doctors swore she would never suffer;
Medication for pain they would buffer.
Auntie Bea began to moan in great pain;
My feelings I could no longer restrain.

~~***~~

I ran down the hall to the nurse station;
I shouted out all of my frustration!
Auntie Bea was not supposed to suffer;
My presence grew angrier and tougher.
Immediately a doctor was called.
I ran back to my auntie, still appalled.

~~***~~

I waited while I held her tight and sighed.
I looked at her closely and did confide,
You know if this is given, what will be?
She said, tell the doctor, give it to me.
He gave her morphine on such a high dose.
Family came and knew time of death was close.

~~***~~

A little black poodle, she always had.
Fe Fe must have lived forty years, not bad.
Fe Fe's came and went, no one said a word;
For it to be the same dog was absurd!
Her poodle was FeFe, no other name.
After all, to her they were all the same.

~~***~~

The last years after the last Fe Fe died,
A German Shepard she cared for with pride.
Killer was older and needed a friend.
On her Smokey, she could always depend.
To me, you were my favorite aunt, Killer.
With you, life was always a big thriller!

~~***~~

The thing I remember about her most,
Was at her table, eating brisket roast.
All those who came into her home, she fed;
To family and friends such joy she spread.
Oh, but beware if she did not like you,
It was clear, away from Killer you drew!

~~***~~

Shedding of a Tear

When flow of love has necessity for flight.
The truth is love cannot co-exist with fright.
Wondrous thoughts transform into feelings of fear,
Bring with it, the constant shedding of a tear.

~~*~~

Kind words can temporarily, help the pain.
Letting answers go, not wanting to feel blame.
A new beginning must ultimately know,
Explanations are necessary to grow.

~~*~~

New choice of words must be put into effect,
Life starting anew; commencing to connect,
We cannot erase what has already been,
We can lay it behind and choose to begin.

~*~

Tropical Storm ...
(Haiku Suite)

A tropical land
storm is brewing with fast winds
palm trees are shaking.

~*~

Ocean is rising
troubled by winds great power
sand will be covered.

~*~

Wind is very strong
palm branches are holding on
gust may pull them off.

~*~

Tropical beauty
may be consumed by a storm
beauty will be gone.

~*~

Beautiful palm trees
tropical winds are forceful
roots clinging for life.

~*~

Some palms have fallen
big storm is destroying trees
fierce winds have power.

~*~

Daveda
(Diamantes)

Daveda
Friendly, Happy
Loving, Forgiving, Caring
Wife, Mother, Trustworthy Friend
Untrusting, Demanding, Risk-taking
Lazy, Arduous
Woman

~*~

The Pictures

It was raining that day, I saw the ladder down.
I paused; then decided to go and take a look.
It was dark, so I stepped very slowly around.
I turned on the dim light; then I spotted the book.

∼∼***∼∼

Watching my steps, I was drawn closer to touch it.
I could see it was old and tattered; dusty too!
Heavy as I lifted it; so I had to sit.
I blew off the dust and saw the cover was blue.

∼∼***∼∼

Opened the cover, curious to check inside;
The book slipped right off my knees and onto the floor.
Many papers fell out, as the book opened wide.
The things I saw and picked up, I could not ignore.

∼∼***∼∼

I sat frozen in time; memories did unfold,
Of a life rapidly passed, a long time ago.
Hopes and dreams of a young girl had never been told,
Now lying here, for me to think back, nice and slow.

~~***~~

Had all these chapters of a life really occurred?
It almost seemed like I'd had a very long dream.
Details gave the impression of having been blurred.
Just could be my imagination, it did seem.

~~***~~

Heaven on Earth

I have a little space, which is just for me.
It is somewhere that I always love to be.
Some place for me, which has a great deal of worth.
Beside my Sonny is my heaven on earth.

In his embrace, there's a sensation so rare,
Based upon a deep love; no one can compare.
Emotions from within bring smiles to my face.
Warmth glows, as my body senses my heart race.

~~***~~

**Two souls destined to be as one forever
My heaven on earth is what I do treasure.
As I gaze into his eyes of azure blue,
My soul comes alive with a love ever true.**

~~***~~

**I have arrived where I have so longed to be.
My own heaven on earth is my destiny.
Close to the man, who does make me feel alive.
Together we stand, as both of us do thrive.**

~~***~~

We Cannot Forget

September, I went to Erie PA.
My husband had a meeting there that day.
Driving back, it took one and a half hours.
In the car, we both watched the rain showers.

^^*^*

Waiting was a message, from my daughter.
At her college, there was a big slaughter.
She lost her cell phone, with my cell number.
Her sad feelings, she did not encumber.

^^*^*

The entrance that she uses everyday;
Was in a complete state of disarray.
A shooter had shot teenagers, many;
The news was then saying, maybe twenty.

^^*^*

She has not been injured, physically;
But, who knows what scars she has mentally.
I thank God that my daughter is alive;
But, there are others, who did not survive.

^^*^*

Over this sad news, I am still upset.
Of school shootings, I will never forget.
All over, there is so much despair.
For the families, please help and say a prayer.

^^*^*

Shari the Lionhearted
To Sharon ...my sister ...whose body has never been found...

When you handed me that last birthday card,
I never knew it would be all so hard.
Well wishes to me that came from your heart,
With dreams that we would never be apart.
You never stopped breaking all of the rules,
We thought it was a joke on April Fools.

~~*~~

It was April first; you went out that day.
I called mommy, we both felt the same way.
Feeling something was wrong deep in my heart,
Mommy and I did not know where to start.
The police were no help and did not care.
Only thing I could do was say a prayer.

There was nothing to give us any hope.
We were finding it very hard to cope.
Police say you were murdered, but not found.
They say dumped off a bridge or in the ground.
Little sister, I almost lost my mind.
My wish is that, you could just send me a sign.

~~*~~

Sister, I keep your pictures and the card.
I know my heart will be forever be scarred.
Rest in peace sister, wherever you are.
If I knew, I'd come; no matter how far,
Your body now no longer has a face,
I dream of you covered in fine white lace.

~~*~~

Each year when the month of April begins,
I do try to forgive those who have sinned.
No grave and no closure, it hurts us so.
This, our burden, forever we will tow.
Shari The Lion Hearted, just feel freed!
Oh Lord, forgive those who have done this deed.

~~*~~

You Will Never Rule Me
(French Ballade)

Nice when you bring me a flower.
Such gestures are so very sweet.
Minutes turn into an hour,
Time with you, is a lovely treat.
This heart of mine does skip a beat.
With you, I desire to be free.
Together, can we be complete?
Dear Prince, you will never rule me.

~~*~~

Gifts on me, you always shower.
With a smile for you, I will greet.
I step slowly from my tower,
As my body builds up with heat.
I must attempt to be discreet.
Fear within me, he shall not see.
I may have to plan my retreat.
Dear Prince, you will never rule me.

~~*~~

To your will, I will not cower.
Beside me, you may have a seat.
I insist on having power.
Listen well, I will not repeat,
I shall not grovel at you feet.
So what, if you do not agree?
Demands, I will by no means meet.
Dear Prince, you will never rule me.

~~*~~

My decision will be concrete.
I will not listen, if you plea.
I suggest, you admit defeat.
Dear Prince, you will never rule me.

~~*~~

*authors note French Ballade: syllable count
remains the same for each line ...
3- 8-line stanzas rhyming ababbcbC, ...
followed by a 4-line envoi rhyming bcbC ...
the same rhymes being used throughout ...
the upper case C's indicate that the same line
is repeated at the end of each stanza ...
these days, the envoi
(last stanza that wraps up the poem)
is addressed to Prince ...
generally understood to be the Prince of Darkness

~*~

Render a Vow

**In the blink of an eye, two years have gone by.
I shed many tears, but now my eyes are dry.
As I gaze to the sky, I know in my heart,
It was deemed we were not meant to be apart.**

~~*~~

Difficult times and agony we withstood,
Others in our place, certainly never could.
My tolerance gets tested some of the time,
Words, from my mouth, leave the taste of bitter wine.

~~*~~

Yet a sensation of peace can overcome;
When in your arms, we sense that we are as one.
Souls sharing a unity of true love,
A variety others, just whisper of.

~~*~~

Come, hold my hand and render a vow to me.
The same one, as the night, you knelt on one knee.
When you searched into my eyes and asked with pride;
I answered yes; I do want to be your bride.

~*~

Happy Mother's Day
(Acrostic-Rhymed) To my mother, **Sonia**...

Having a mother like you,
Always knowing your heart was true.
Pleasing your children the best you could,
Proudly making gourmet meals, oh so good.
Yummy things, no one else had!

Making us feel better when we were sad;
Overworking yourself, to give us more.
Telling us not, when you felt sore.
Hiding when you were in pain,
Even, when you waited for a bus, in the rain.
Remembering to make our lunches for school,
Sending the best for us, for you are a jewel.

Dearest mommy, this daughter knows,
A mother like you is a beautiful rose.
You are the reason, my love just grows!

Mother's Day

to my mother ...Sonia

Mom
So calm
Loving me
Since I was wee
I give you my heart
Although we are apart
On you Mom I can depend
You will always be my best friend
I care for you and hope it does show
Love for you each day continues to grow

<<<<<<<<>>>>>><<<<<<<>>>>>>>*

There is nothing better that you can find
Than my loving Mom who is so kind
Even with things I put you through
Mom the love you show is true
My mom I must convey
Happy Mother's Day
Wishes are due
I love you
My dear
Mom

Dear Santa

A letter from the little girl in me...

Dear Santa, I want to make my wishes clear,
By explaining, what I need from you this year.
It would be nice to have a world without fear,
Wonderful if no one had to shed a tear!

****

For me, really I do not need very much.
My requirements are not those you can touch,
I am asking for health, to those who are sick,
If you can, would you do that for me, Saint Nick?

****

To the hungry people, would you bring some food?
Maybe something tasty, Mrs. Clause has stewed.
Can you give shelter, to all those without beds?
Lead them to a place, to lay their weary heads.

****

Santa, make all wars end, I implore of you.
To those with hate in their hearts, give them a clue.
I ask, please, help the children who are abused.
Help the good people, so they would not be used.

****

Santa, help the world be the land of the free;
You will not have to buy anything for me.
I know that by now, you are giving a yawn,
I'll try not to make my list go on and on!

What Children Say

When my children were young I tried to teach;
The signs along the road, I showed them each.
Pictures and words, I would show them to see,
So, that they could match them, to some degree.

Shop that sold doors had a picture of one.
They yelled, "They sell doors!" learning had begun.
Jewelry stores; my daughter loved to see.
She always asked, "Will you buy some for me?"

Shoe stores would have a picture of a shoe.
Children were learning to spell as they grew.
When they saw food on the sign they would yell,
"Mommy, look a restaurant; I can spell"

One day we drove to the shopping center,
I had intentions for us to enter.
My son, with eyes wide, at the sign did stare.
He screamed, "They be selling donkeys in there!"

My daughter, then to her sibling, did smirk,
"There are no donkeys; is your mind berserk?"
Having children made my life full of joy.
I came alive watching my girl and boy!

True Love
(English Cameo)

Loving

Another deeply

Gives ones heart happiness so pure

Feeling loved

Makes life peaceful and lets us dream

True love lasting forever

Just right

Mirror of Me

Who is that pretty lady standing there?
A rose blooming with an essence so rare,
Familiar are the eyes she looks into.
She knows that she is part of life anew.

A mother looks into her daughter's eyes,
Reflections of herself begin to rise.
She stares and thinks back; she can plainly see,
She says, "Child you are a mirror of me."

~~*~~

The child, now a mother, looks at a face.
Her daughter she picks up and does embrace.
A daughter looks at her mother and smiles,
As the mother starts to think, how time flies.

~~*~~

Another daughter becomes a mother.
Her child sees that she looks like another.
A grandmother has passed on something rare,
A beautiful face, for one more to share.

~~*~~

A mother looks into her daughter's eyes,
Reflections of herself begin to rise.
She stares and thinks back; she can plainly see,
She says, "Child you are a mirror of me."

Flowers from A Friend

Doorbell rang; I went to see who was there.
A man was standing with flowers so fair.
"Are you Daveda?" the nice man asked me.
"Yes that is I, but from whom can they be?"

He handed me a basket with a card.
This gift had caught me completely off guard!
I read the card carefully; then I cried.
Wonderful feelings it gave me inside!

> THANKS FOR BEING THERE FOR ME.
> THINKIING OF YOU AND HOPE YOUR ARE
> FEELING GOOD. SO MUCH LOOKING
> FORWARD TO SEEING YOU IN TORONTO.
> PRAYING FOR YOU TO BE BLESSED
> ALWAYS.
> YOUR FRIEND,
> PAT

Delighted I am, to have a great friend.
Pat Simpson brightened up my whole weekend!
I am certain there are of angels around,
Some have wings, others with us, earth bound!

*authors note ...my friend Pat is the world renowned author Patricia Ann Farnsworth-Simpson

Happy Birthday Pat!

Who is the greatest lady we know?
Cannot guess, then I will have to show.
She writes all kinds of poems so great.
One of the finest you'll find, I state!

She writes and puts her heart into much;
Pat's always around to keep in touch.
Charity books for kids, she puts out.
A lady we could not do without!

Put her at laptop and let her roll.
A lady she is, with a good soul.
If by chance you do not know her face;
You might be sitting in outer space!

Happy Birthday Pat, my special friend.
You are just stuck with me, till the end.
Dear lady with a heart of pure gold;
Read her work, let her beauty unfold!

^V^

Four Letters

It is something that can be big or small,
You can obtain one or two at the mall.
It can take you to a far away place.
Some of them can really make your heart race.

>>>***<<<

I have many, which I own, in my house.
There are those; which I have shared with my spouse.
There's some that keep me busy for a while!
Many of them tend to help make me smile.

>>>***<<<

Some new ones make me think about my friends.
They can be what another recommends!
There are those I hang on to, though they're torn.
Some special ones tend to look pretty worn.

>>>***<<<

Everyone is different as can be,
Within some, realty I can see.
Others can make me forget where I am,
In the past; helped me cram for an
exam.

>>>***<<<

Have an idea of what I can be?
If you don't, would you really want to see?
This is easy, let's all take a long look,
Of what can be inside of a good
book!

>>>***<<<

The Mirror

When did you realize things were not so good?
What makes you sense you are misunderstood?
It seems that nothing will make you content.
Why inside are you feeling this torment?

~~*~~

What would turn a woman into a fool?
Why do you believe your life is so cruel?
Did you dream, life could be any better?
The splashes of tears cannot be wetter.

~~*~~

Why do you whimper, when all seems sedate?
What has made your inner thoughts so irate?
Maybe, anticipations were not found.
Loneliness stays, when others are around.

~~*~~

Thoughts won't stop tumbling around in your head.
Could it be the fear of what lies ahead?
The sobs, from deep within, cannot be heard.
Reality has made this life absurd.

~~*~~

Where are you, now, my friend in the mirror?
Can you tell me how to make it clearer?
As you fade into someone I don't know,
I must now learn if you are friend or foe.

~*~

By Your Side

to Debra

I know your situation is difficult right now,
Still, it will only do to you; what you will allow.

∼∼***∼∼

You have talent and charm, my wonderful friend.
My caring for you; I will always extend.

∼∼***∼∼

Your heart is filled with righteousness and love,
Qualities, I sometimes remind you of.

∼∼***∼∼

Stand tall and chose the path that is right for you.
Whatever you decide, you must see it through.

~~***~~

I will be by your side, though I am far away.
Please, know I think about you each and every day.

~~***~~

Birthdays come and birthdays go,
This one will be hard, I know.

~~***~~

Keep in mind, the future will be bright.
Now, you have learned and have more insight.

~~***~~

Self love is the first love, which you must fight to find.
Then can you give and receive love and be entwined.

~~***~~

Happy birthday my dear friend; remember I care.
Enjoy your day, in my heart, with you I am there.

~***~

A Friend like You
(Acrostic-Rhymed)

As we grow, good friends are harder to find.

Familiarity is important; for lives to be entwined.
Realities of friendship lead us to know,
Integrity in others has reached a new plateau.
Earnestly, we strive to find others we can trust;
Nobly and ever trying not to be unjust.
Determined we were, to discover a special friend.

Lynn, as our friendship began to transcend;
In a few short days; I knew that I was blessed.
Kindred spirits we are; to that I can attest;
Essentially, knowing that we both agree.

You and I, most certainly hold a special key;
Offering each other, a friendship beyond compare.
Understanding the sacred gift we both can share!

Open Your Mind
(Italian Ottava Rima)

Keep moving forward,
it is the only way.
Bad recollections
are to leave in the past.
Dwell upon them;
they will never go away.
Cast gloomy thoughts aside;
they can be surpassed,
If you like,
glimpse ahead for a brighter day.
Heed my words;
the future is on its way fast.
Happiness can come,
just open up your mind.
Your actions will determine
what you will find.

~*~

Scorpio Season
(October 24-November 22)

Scorpio season will commence on this day.
We feel anew and want to come out to play.
There are strong senses of sexual desires.
Some of you, of my story, are not buyers!

>>>***<<<

Wait and you will see what begins to take place.
Is that a flush of red I see on your face?
The sensual awareness you start to feel,
Do you question me; is this not a big deal?

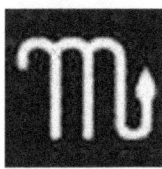

Feel almighty fire you have been longing for.
As it takes over, you'll be craving for more.
Let your body become totally aroused,
A lack of it; for much too long, has be housed.

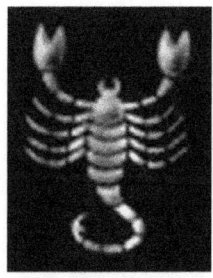

**Do you have a lover to share raging fire?
Give in to the flame of uncovered desire.
Find the yearning, which brews and bubbles within.
This unique time of year will swiftly begin.**

**As the bodies of those in love, are entwined.
The ecstasy will begin to blow your mind.
Shout your emotions of passion to the moon.
Scorpio season will be over too soon!**

>>>***<<<

Who I Am
(Acrostic-Rhymed)

Difficult to tell you, what makes me who I am;
A woman who wants to know as much as she can.
Voicing my opinion is something I couldn't stop;
Endeavoring relentlessly, to get to the top.
Desiring constantly to be first-rate at what I do;
Always giving a good shot; whatever I go through.

>>>***<<<

Giving love freely, because I genuinely care;
Ready to give anyone who needs one, a prayer.
Unique in my style, I have to be who I am;
Believing in myself, even if it gets me in a jam.
Ever wanting loyalty from those close to me;
Remembering who gives it and who doesn't agree.

>>>***<<<

Love in America

Daveda

found

love and marriage

from looking at a distance

to

America

Our delicious desire

is found in our love

sharing

yesterday

today

and tomorrow!

>>>***<<<

Marriage (Pentaphor)

Couple must feel love
Each show affection
Both want devotion
Care for each other
In good and bad health

~~*~~

Use loving words
Have tender touch
Kiss with meaning
Share time alone

~~*~~

Be best friends
Never stray
From partner

~~*~~

Closeness
Gives you

~~*~~
Love
~*~

The Brilliance of Love
To the sunrise in my life ....Sonny

Daveda

found

the brilliance of love

unfolding delicious desire

for

Sonny

~~~*^*^*^*~~~

The sunrise had

awaken in me

daylight found

I was thinking

of delicious desire

with you, my love

~~*^*^*~~

Such Love
(Rictometer)

~*~
Sonny
Love of my life
He gives me all I need
A man who shows how much he cares
Such a charming man so handsome to see
Someone with whom I share such love
I give thanks everyday
I love you so
Sonny
~*~

For Eternity

**Fingers slowly
moving on my
long silky hair
my eyes closed
my body
is hot
with desire
for his love**

~~^^^^^^~~

**Our eyes meet
delicious desire
is found alive
beautifully in love
we will be for**

Eternity

~^^^~

Take Me Away

As I stare, into the abyss, in front of me,
I ask myself, is this, what has been planned to be?
Where are all the hues of bright blue that I once saw?
Is the sight of the outdoors, which makes me withdraw?

~~<<>>*<<>>~~

There are so many questions mixed up in my head;
Alas, I feel the answers are those that I dread.
I have asked those in high places; to no avail;
Will the persistence in me, once again prevail?

~~<<>>*<<>>~~

I shudder to think, yes, I will go back again.
The thought of this optimism drives me insane.
Please, I beg, someone take me away from this place!
As I dream for an answer, I stare into space.

I sadly look, as I shake my head in despair.
It certainly appears; I am glued to this chair.
Will I dare stop looking at a computer screen?
I think I am doomed; I really need some caffeine!

~<<>>*<<>>~

Hopes For You ...(Ottava Rima)

It has come the time, for you to be a man.
Your family has always had hopes for you;
Graduating High School has been the grand plan.
You're family, proud as they watched how you grew,
College, only a dream when your life began.
Now, comes the greatest choice that you can pursue.
There comes a time when you can go for the gold.
The payoff will be as you watch life unfold!

Souls Entwined

A man stood on the bridge, looking at the river below.
He could see in his reflection; his face was all aglow.
Had he lived a million lifetimes, in this short span of time?
He was getting older, but felt like he was in his prime.

∼∼*^*^*^*^*∼∼

The currents of water flowed quickly, like the time had passed.
In the autumn of his life, had he found true love at last?
He reminisced, and in the water, her face he could see.
Through his own reflection, her beauty helped to set him free.

Feeling at that very instant, he so wanted her love.
Understanding that a love as this; was sent from above.
The yellow moon shimmered upon the river as it shined.
At that very moment in time, he felt their souls entwined.

Hearts Aglow

Love is caring for each other, in so many ways.
A love enduring, it has lasted through every phase.
Young love, has brought a couple together, long ago.
Sixty-five years have past, but still, their hearts are aglow.

They brought to life four children, who, through the years have grown.
There are three of them, who are not friends, who, I have known.
One daughter to Herb and Ginny is special to me.
Lynn is a wonderful woman, of that, we agree.

She invited me here, to honor her mom and dad.
Lynn thinks they are a special couple; that I may add.
A marriage with a history of sixty-five years,
Herb and Ginny did something right; that surely appears.

So, this day of celebration is meant for these two.
We can learn from this fine couple, how love stayed and grew.
Hold up a glass and give a toast of cheer, on this day.
Herb and Ginny, we certainly admire you today!

* authors note
my friend Lynn had a party for her parents 65th Wedding Anniversary her mom loves daisies ...she asked if I would write a poem and read it

As She Gazed

A woman stood on the rocks, looking out to sea.
Could she find the answer here; had she found the key?
Titanic went down, into the waters so cold,
She saw the movie and how the story was told.

She loves her daughter, from the bottom of her heart.
You are in heaven, so, for now you are apart.
She is sad, because she cannot go to your grave.
It hurts her, that her own daughter, she could not save.

~~<<>>*<<>>~~

She gazes to the water and feels a cold chill.
For life, you had not the gift of hope or the will.
She wonders, you watched the movie; what reason why,
Did you have to watch, and see so much death and die?

Immigration

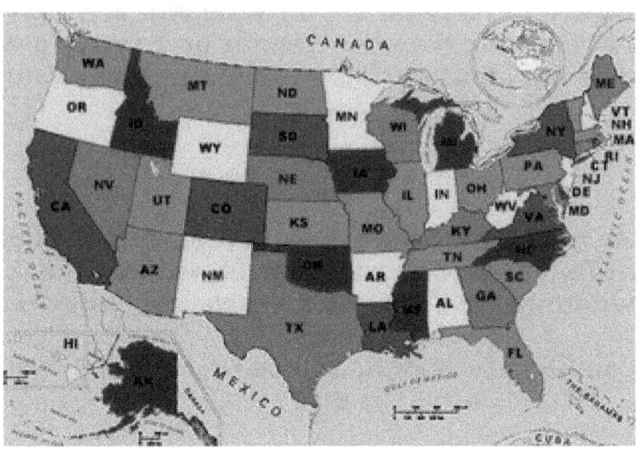

There will be an election in the U.S.A.
This one will mean more than others, I must convey.
Recently I've become a US resident.
Now, I care more, about who will be president.

~~?~~

Everything was legally done to get married.
A financial burden; my husband carried.
I am from Canada, a country so close by,
Those from Mexico don't seem to have to apply.

~~?~~

In the state of Texas, my girlfriend got married.
It seems as though the rules state to state are varied.
My friend is a Canadian, the same as me,
In Texas things are run rather differently.

~~?~~

No need for a fiancée's visa, to be wed.
She just got her legal papers after, instead.
We are both legal residents in the US,
Only, I had to go through so much of a mess.

∼∼?∼∼

What would it take to get into Canada, now?
While paying attention, I tend to raise my brow.
Women coming through customs and immigration,
Hair and face covered, who walks into this nation?

∼∼?∼∼

Should not immigration be the same for us all?
Equality in Canada; what I recall.
In the U.S.A., I can see this is not true.
To find it in Canada, sure makes me feel blue.

∼∼?∼∼

My face is shown on my Canadian passport.
Traveling with face covered. I do not support.
When can it be, what's good for one is good for all?
I hope to experience it, before we fall!

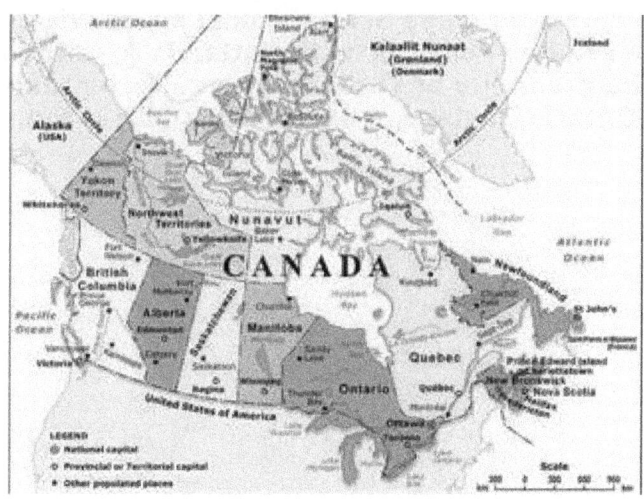

For The Future

I have witnessed such beauty in the things I see,
Relishing in the glory knowing I am free.
From Montreal, the unique city, of my birth,
Memories everlasting; having so much worth.

I remember Nova Scotia's most scenic views,
The Prairie Provinces with flatlands to enthuse;
The great city of Toronto with culture grand;
Ontario, a place, where I can again stand.

~~<<>>*<<>>~~

Now, I live in the magnificent U.S.A.
Have seen mystique of Hawaii, I can say.
The splendor of California, I have been to.
Beaches of Florida, with sun shining bright blue.

Florida   Hawaii >

Bustling cities, like New York and Boston, I've viewed.
Philadelphia and Pittsburgh, I must include.
I've had the joy to visit so many places,
Now, living in PA, with wide-open spaces.

Will my children and grandchildren be able to,
Be as fortunate, to see the world as I do?
It is up to common people like me and you,
So, help to save the land, for the future to view!

It Won't Get Me!

One day in the cold month of November,
No way that I could ever remember;
Many rejoiced as love flowed out to me.
Wishes, a good woman; one day I'd be.

~~*~~

The roads chosen have not always been right,
When it was needed, I fought the good fight.
As my trails of life began to get rough,
I answered with all my strength and got tough.

~~*~~

When my tears flowed like rivers, as I cried,
I wiped them quickly, that can't be denied.
From what is thrown at me, I will not hide.
The strength that is needed, God will provide.

~~*~~

If this new battle tries to bring me down,
I won't permit weakness to be around.
Difficulties in my life won't get me.
I'll fight to the end; that I guarantee!

Road of Life

As I travel the road of life.
I recede to look at the strife.
For the places I have been to,
The hardships, which I have gone through,
Have shown to me the shinning light.
Good and bad, also wrong and right.

~~*~~

A daughter was taken from me;
Now, trust in God is what I see.
My sister was murdered, I know,
Still, I must continue to grow.
Although her body was not found,
Never laid to rest in the ground.

~~*~~

Abuse is no stranger to me.
I have found the way to break free.
I will not hold hate in my heart;
To let it go; is to be smart.
Holding hate is for the coward.
Forgiveness makes you empowered.

~*~

Myself (Rictometer)

Myself,
As I perceive,
Is hard for some to see.
Looking at me for the first time,
I can appear as unapproachable.
In fact I am very friendly
And generous, as well.
I even like
Myself.

~<<>>*<<>>~

Ones Worth

I have met certain people along the road of life.
The ones that harbor hate within the depths of their soul,
Will be those who inevitably subsist with strife.
For they have permitted hatred to seize all control.

∼∼*∼∼

As they attempt to push forward into the future,
Their minds engulfed with judgments that they cannot explain.
Those who hold on to the wicked thoughts that they nurture;
They uncaringly unleash insufferable pain.

∼∼*∼∼

Undeniable nasty thoughts are for the coward.
There is a much wiser way to survive on this earth.
To be able to forgive is to be empowered.
What one does for others is what determines ones worth.

The Book

Book
(Acrostic-Rhymed)

Beyond the fantasies in my head;
Overlooking a world of what I read.
Ordinary things can make life bright,
Keeping them for me to delight!

>>>***<<<

Desired Splendor

My mind travels to uncharted heights;
A journey upward, my heart takes flight.

^^*^*^*^*

So tall, I stretch to kiss his lips of wine.
A murmur in my head; tells me he is mine.

^^*^*^*^*

An arduous task for me to conceive;
That the day would come that I would believe.

^^*^*^*^*

A gentle man with a love so tender;
I have found in him, such desired splendor.

^^*^*^*^*

I give him my heart, on silver platter.
Without him, I know that my life would shatter.

^^*^*^*^*

I have endured much on the roads traveled,
But, now my life is set and unraveled.

^^*^*^*^*

A gift to me has at last been bestowed.
Through this wondrous reward, true love has flowed.

^^*^*^*^*

This beautiful love is heaven sent;
God has deemed for me to be content.

^^*^*^*^*

I have found in the deep entity of my soul,
Adoration astounding, to make me feel whole.

^^*^*^*^*

I can now see the glory; which dreams are made of.
The reverie came true; I have found my true love.

^^*

Husband and Lover
(Soul mate challenge by Poet and author
Christina R Jussaume)

to my husband ...Sonny

I waited for him
Till he came into my life
He made me his wife

~*~

Lover
One and only
So loving and tender
Making my wildest dreams come true
Giving me passion and true love from you
The love we share is forever
Your love for me is real
Just hold me tight
Lover

~*~

Sonny
Love of my life
He gives me all I need
A man who shows how much he cares
Such a charming man so handsome to see
Someone with whom I share such love
I give thanks everyday
I love you so
Sonny

~*~

My heart did open
For true love to step inside
Now I am his bride

~*~

By way of heaven
God sent to me a rare gift
Sonny is his name

~*~

My Sunshine He Is!

Glasses of Love
...to my Sonny

**Cheers to the world's best
HUSBAND !!!**

**Sonny
and
Daveda
the
Greatest
Love
of
All**

```
**~*~*~*~**     **~*~*~*~**
 *** love***     *** love***
   **~*~**         **~*~**
     *~*             *~*
      l               l
      l               l
      l               l
    =*=*=           =*=*=
```

**I hope you have enjoyed my book,
Thank You! All who have read!
God Bless You!**
Daveda

~*~

Other books by Daveda

Snapshots ...a Blonde View

SoulAsylum Publishers

" Daveda is a woman, wife, mother and poet. This book is full of snapshots from her life, told in rhyme. Daveda's love of life comes shining through, whether she is sharing absurd anecdotes of domestic life, or recounting very personal episodes that would bring many people to despair.

One thing is for certain, she can laugh at herself on this trip through time, and she invites you to come along for the ride. A ride you will not soon forget, so strap yourself in and fly away with Daveda.....

~*~

Tales of a Tiny Dog

By Passion for Poetry Publishers
This book is in full color and has pictures of people and dogs that are a part of her enchanting life. Give the child in your life a real treat. Let them read and see the tales of a tiny dog name Lady Godiva. She is a chocolate teacup poodle that weighs four pounds, full grown; a small but mighty pup that will win any heart! Give the child in your life a real treat. Let them read and see the tales of a tiny dog name Lady Godiva. She is a chocolate teacup poodle that weighs four pounds, full grown; a small but mighty pup that will win any heart!

~*~

Other Books By
Passion For Poetry Publishers

Jack The Lad
Patricia Ann Farnsworth-Simpson

The Wizard, The Witch
&
Joe the Toe
Patricia Ann Farnsworth-Simpson

*^v^*

**Amazing Pets and Animals
Christina R. Jussaume**

*^v^*
The Butter Bee Book

For Children in NEED

*^v^*

Other Children's Charity books
Published by Passion For Poetry

by
Patricia Ann Farnsworth-Simpson
Featuring Daveda and other Poets World-Wide
A compilation of poems and short stories from poets/ authors world-wide! All contributed to produce this book which all the proceeds will go to the Save The Children... it is a wonderful collection of poems and stories that both adults and children will enjoy reading... as all are have been written to show children that with love and understanding you can overcome troubles to stand tall... anyone purchasing this large full color book will get wonderful joy reading and by also having the knowledge that they too have helped raise funds for the kids charity....

*^v^*

by
Patricia Ann Farnsworth-Simpson
Featuring Daveda and Other Poets World-Wide

A delightful book for all children to love and read, one too that will be greatly enjoyed by all who love reading poetry with a story/message written within. This book is like taking a magical journey through life, where love of God triumphs and loving care of children, animals both pets and wild are shown within the pages. A book passionately put together by poets world-wide to give children pleasure and encourage them to read more, but also to help raise funds for sick children in need as every author taking part as donated their work and their share of royalties to this very worthy cause... The Sick Children's Hospital in Toronto!

*^v^*

www.ingramcontent.com/pod-product-compliance
Lightning Source LLC
Chambersburg PA
CBHW032005080426
42735CB00007B/510